Life Changing Quotes

for

Teachers
Education,
and
Learning.

David Sparks

Copyright © 2015 David Sparks

All Rights Reserved

Contents

Introduction 5
Section 1 **Teachers** 7
Section 2 **Education** 32
Section 3 **Learning** 92

Introduction

Quotes seem to have a magical quality about them. For some reason, many people love reading them. Maybe it's because the words speak to the person or maybe because they like and admire the author. Either way, quotes seem to carry an energy of their own, like a call to action.

Quotes can be inspirational to many, however just as many are not inspired. This may have to do with timing. When a reader reads a quote, they may not be in the appropriate state of mind, or the appropriate stage in their life to appreciate the meaning or lessons behind the words.

As a teacher I have displayed quite a few quotes around my classroom with the hope that one of them will inspire the students and motivate them to work that little bit harder. I was truly amazed when I received a phone call from parents of a student, thanking me for what I had said in class one day. These parents had been having difficulty with their 15-year-old son for quite some time, but he did a turn around after reading one of the new quotes I had put up in the room. The quote was **"time is all you've got and time is running out."** I had heard it while listening to a Jim Rohn tape and thought it would be useful to the students, as school would finish before they knew it.

The quotes written in this book are specifically about Teachers, Education and Learning. Everyone has an opinion on these areas, probably because of its political and social importance, but also because of experiences individuals have had, either as teachers or students.

One thing many of the authors seem to be in accordance with is that the best and most important lessons are learned through living and doing. Not everything can be taught in a classroom, and everyone is not ready at the same time to learn. I guess the old Buddhist proverb is correct that **"When the student is ready the teacher will appear."**

The words in this book come from actors and actresses, athletes, businessmen and women, politicians, musicians, philosophers, scientists and more. Some quotes go back as far as ancient Rome and ancient Greece and are still relevant to this day.

I suggest this book be used as a regular 'go to', so keep it handy and look at it often. You may read something now which may not resonate with you at this point in your life, but a year or two down the track, it will have a totally different meaning.

You will notice that a few quotes sound the same, but come from different authors. I have put this down to the individuals being on the same wavelength and their experiences having led them to formulate similar beliefs.

Of course, you probably won't find every quote useful or inspiring, but this is to be expected. Since everyone's values are different, different quotations will inspire different people.

Hopefully you will enjoy these quotes for a long time to come and notice the improvements that benefit your life by making the small changes that these sages provoke.

Teachers

A child's first teacher is its mother.
— **Peng Liyuan**

A good teacher can inspire hope, ignite the imagination, and instil a love of learning.
— **Brad Henry**

A good teacher, like a good entertainer first must hold his audience's attention, then he can teach his lesson.
— **John Henrik Clarke**

A teacher affects eternity; he can never tell where his influence stops.
— **Henry Adams**

Teachers can change lives with just the right mix of chalk and challenges.
— **Joyce Meyer**

The one exclusive sign of thorough knowledge is the power of teaching.
— **Aristotle**

Experience is a good teacher, but she sends in terrific bills.
- Minna Antrim

Failure is a great teacher, and I think when you make mistakes and you recover from them and you treat them as valuable learning experiences, then you've got something to share.
- Steve Harvey

One good teacher in a lifetime may sometimes change a delinquent into a solid citizen.
- Philip Wylie

The dream begins with a teacher who believes in you, who tugs and pushes and leads you to the next plateau, sometimes poking you with a sharp stick called 'truth'.
- Dan Rather

The task of the modern educator is not to cut down jungles, but to irrigate deserts.
- C. S. Lewis

Good teachers know how to bring out the best in students.
- Charles Kuralt

If I am walking with two other men, each of them will serve as my teacher. I will pick out the good points of the one and imitate them, and the bad points of the other and correct them in myself.

- Confucius

It is the supreme art of the teacher to awaken joy in creative expression and knowledge.

- Albert Einstein

Education is the key to success in life, and teachers make a lasting impact in the lives of their students.

- Solomon Ortiz

One looks back with appreciation to the brilliant teachers, but with gratitude to those who touched our human feelings. The curriculum is so much necessary raw material, but warmth is the vital element for the growing plant and for the soul of the child.

- Carl Jung

Every child should have a caring adult in their lives. And that's not always a biological parent or family member. It may be a friend or neighbor. Often times it is a teacher.

- Joe Manchin

I have come to believe that a great teacher is a great artist and that there are as few as there are any other great artists. Teaching might even be the greatest of the arts since the medium is the human mind and spirit.
- **John Steinbeck**

I think the teaching profession contributes more to the future of our society than any other single profession.
- **John Wooden**

The art of teaching is the art of assisting discovery.
- **Mark Van Doren**

If you have to put someone on a pedestal, put teachers. They are society's heroes.
- **Guy Kawasaki**

There are two kinds of teachers: the kind that fill you with so much quail shot that you can't move, and the kind that just gives you a little prod behind and you jump to the skies.
- **Robert Frost**

Excellence is a better teacher than mediocrity. The lessons of the ordinary are everywhere. Truly profound and original insights are to be found only in studying the exemplary.
— **Warren Bennis**

We can teach a lot of things, but if the teacher can't relate by talking to a group of friendly students, he'll never be a competent teacher.
— **William Glasser**

My heart is singing for joy this morning! A miracle has happened! The light of understanding has shone upon my little pupil's mind, and behold, all things are changed!
— **Anne Sullivan**

I am indebted to my father for living, but to my teacher for living well.
— **Alexander the Great**

I cannot emphasize enough the importance of a good teacher.
— **Temple Grandin**

The five steps in teaching an employee new skills are preparation, explanation, showing, observation and supervision.

- Bruce Barton

In a completely rational society, the best of us would be teachers and the rest of us would have to settle for something else.

- Lee Iacocca

Most of us end up with no more than five or six people who remember us. Teachers have thousands of people who remember them for the rest of their lives.

- Andy Rooney

I like a teacher who gives you something to take home to think about besides homework.

- Lily Tomlin

A teacher who is attempting to teach without inspiring the pupil with a desire to learn is hammering on cold iron.

- Horace Mann

I saw as a teacher how, if you take that spark of learning that those children have, and you ignite it, you can take a child from any background to a lifetime of creativity and accomplishment.

- **Paul Wellstone**

Those who know how to think need no teachers.

- **Mahatma Gandhi**

A teacher must believe in the value and interest of his subject as a doctor believes in health.

- **Gilbert Highet**

We spend the first twelve months of our children's lives teaching them to walk and talk and the next twelve telling them to sit down and shut up.

- **Phyllis Diller**

The most important part of teaching is to teach what it is to know.

- **Simone Weil**

The best CEOs I know are teachers, and at the core of what they teach is strategy.

- **Michael Porter**

To this end the greatest asset of a school is the personality of the teacher.

- John Strachan

Everybody's a teacher if you listen.

- Doris Roberts

I touch the future. I teach.

- Christa McAuliffe

Your best teacher is your last mistake.

- Ralph Nader

When we become a really mature, grown-up, wise society, we will put teachers at the center of the community, where they belong. We don't honor them enough, we don't pay them enough.

- Charles Kuralt

A teacher should have maximal authority, and minimal power.

- Thomas Szasz

It is the malady of our age that the young are so busy teaching us that they have no time left to learn.
- Eric Hoffer

A true teacher defends his students against his own personal influences.
- Amos Bronson Alcott

A teacher is a person who never says anything once.
- Howard Nemerov

Only one person in a million becomes enlightened without a teacher's help.
- Bodhidharma

A self-taught man usually has a poor teacher and a worse student.
- Henny Youngman

I would suggest that teachers show their students concrete examples of the negative effects of the actions that gangsta rappers glorify.
- Kareem Abdul-Jabbar

We expert teachers know that motivation and emotional impact are what matter.
- **Donald Norman**

TV is bigger than any story it reports. It's the greatest teaching tool since the printing press.
- **Fred W. Friendly**

For the longest time, you just sound like a broken record, but you have to be consistent when teaching kids.
- **Heidi Klum**

If a country is to be corruption free and become a nation of beautiful minds, I strongly feel there are three key societal members who can make a difference. They are the father, the mother and the teacher.
- **A. P. J. Abdul Kalam**

Let us remember: One book, one pen, one child, and one teacher can change the world.
- **Malala Yousafzai**

The greatest sign of success for a teacher... is to be able to say, 'The children are now working as if I did not exist.'
- **Maria Montessori**

The mediocre teacher tells. The good teacher explains. The superior teacher demonstrates. The great teacher inspires.
- **William Arthur Ward**

If you improve a teacher's self-esteem, confidence, communication skills or stress levels, you improve that teacher's overall effectiveness across the curriculum.
- **Elaine MacDonald**

A good teacher must be able to put himself in the place of those who find learning hard.
- **Eliphas Levi**

Experience is the teacher of all things.
- **Julius Caesar**

I have learned that, although I am a good teacher, I am a much better student, and I was blessed to learn valuable lessons from my students on a daily basis. They taught me the importance of teaching to a student - and not to a test.
- **Erin Gruwell**

Music when healthy, is the teacher of perfect order, and when depraved, the teacher of perfect disorder.
- **John Ruskin**

Failure should be our teacher, not our undertaker. Failure is delay, not defeat. It is a temporary detour, not a dead end. Failure is something we can avoid only by saying nothing, doing nothing, and being nothing.
- **Denis Waitley**

A good teacher who can take the zero pay and help kids develop physically, emotionally, socially, is literally an angel.
- **Eva Amurri**

I do believe that when your child does poorly on a test, your first step should not necessarily be to attack the teacher or the school's curriculum. It should be to look at the idea that, maybe, the child didn't work hard enough.
- **Amy Chua**

But the fact is, no matter how good the teacher, how small the class, how focused on quality education the school may be none of this matters if we ignore the individual needs of our students.
- **Roy Barnes**

A teacher should have a creative mind.
- **A. P. J. Abdul Kalam**

If you become a teacher, by your pupils you'll be taught.
- **Oscar Hammerstein II**

The single most important thing in a child's performance is the quality of the teacher. Making sure a child spends the maximum amount of time with inspirational teachers is the most important thing.
- **Michael Gove**

In schools with a history of chaos, the teacher who can keep the classroom calm becomes virtually indispensable.
- **Jonathan Kozol**

The object of teaching a child is to enable him to get along without his teacher.
- **Elbert Hubbard**

It's the teacher that makes the difference, not the classroom.
- **Michael Morpurgo**

Experience is a hard teacher because she gives the test first, the lesson afterward.
- **Vernon Law**

No bubble is so iridescent or floats longer than that blown by the successful teacher.
- **William Osler**

What students lack in school is an intellectual relationship or conversation with the teacher.
- **William Glasser**

I've learned that mistakes can often be as good a teacher as success.
- **Jack Welch**

So what does a good teacher do? Create tension - but just the right amount.
- **Donald Norman**

I have always believed that 98% of a student's progress is due to his own efforts, and 2% to his teacher.
- **John Philip Sousa**

I've got a friend who is a lion tamer. He used to be a school teacher till he lost his nerve.
- **Les Dawson**

Time is a great teacher, but unfortunately it kills all its pupils.

— **Hector Berlioz**

Therefore, a person should first be changed by a teacher's instructions, and guided by principles of ritual. Only then can he observe the rules of courtesy and humility, obey the conventions and rules of society, and achieve order.

— **Xun Zi**

A master can tell you what he expects of you. A teacher, though, awakens your own expectations.

— **Patricia Neal**

There is nothing more valuable than great classroom instruction. But let's stop putting the whole burden on teachers. We also need better parents. Better parents can make every teacher more effective.

— **Thomas Friedman**

Adversity is a great teacher, but this teacher makes us pay dearly for its instruction; and often the profit we derive, is not worth the price we paid.

— **Elizabeth Hardwick**

I'm embarrassed every time I look a teacher in the eye, because we ask them to do so much for so little.
- Phil McGraw

A little girl who finds a puzzle frustrating might ask her busy mother (or teacher) for help. The child gets one message if her mother expresses clear pleasure at the request and quite another if mommy responds with a curt 'Don't bother me - I've got important work to do.'
- Daniel Goleman

I can't tell you how many people say they were turned off from science because of a science teacher that completely sucked out all the inspiration and enthusiasm they had for the course.
- Neil deGrasse Tyson

Benevolence alone will not make a teacher, nor will learning alone do it. The gift of teaching is a peculiar talent, and implies a need and a craving in the teacher himself.
- John Jay Chapman

Tragedy is a hell of a teacher. It's much too strict, but it's a hell of a teacher.
- Harlan Coben

Being a teacher is back-breakingly difficult work. It is also extremely important work.

- Timothy Noah

I'd like to say I was smart enough to finish six grades in five years, but I think perhaps the teacher was just glad to get rid of me.

- Alan Shepard

Knowing what to expect from a teacher is a really good thing, of course: It lets you get the right answers more quickly than you would otherwise.

- Alison Gopnik

There are moments as a teacher when I'm conscious that I'm trotting out the same exact phrase my professor used with me years ago. It's an eerie feeling, as if my old mentor is not just in the room, but in my shoes, using me as his mouthpiece.

- Abraham Verghese

In a home school, the kid does 95% of the work. But in a school system, since it's an indoctrination system, a teacher has to do 95% of the work.

- John Taylor Gatto

Teacher compensation isn't the only factor in cultivating great teaching. Other important priorities include changing how we measure student performance, providing more flexibility to teacher-preparation programs, and improving how we train and support principals.

- Michael Bennet

The best teacher is an entertainer.

- Bob Keeshan

Children are already accustomed to a world that moves faster and is more exciting than anything a teacher in front of a classroom can do.

- Major Owens

As a teacher you can see the difference in kids who have parents who were involved. That difference, by the time these kids get to the third grade, is drastic.

- Jenna Bush

The teacher, who would be true to his mission and accomplish the most good, must give prominence to moral as well as intellectual instruction.

- Sheldon Jackson

If we can teach a teacher we can reach more people.
> **- Richard Stengel**

All it takes is one teacher - just one - to save us from ourselves and make us forget all the others.
> **- Daniel Pennac**

I am a teacher born and bred, and I believe in the advocacy of teachers. It's a calling. We want our students to feel impassioned and empowered.
> **- Erin Gruwell**

I always thought I would be a teacher. And I think I actually lived up to my initial dreams, because what I do now is teach millions and millions of people many different kinds of things.
> **- Martha Stewart**

The teacher is commodified, the school is a shop, the subjects are consumer goods. To read, to think, to reflect, isn't a question of want, it's a question of need.
> **- Daniel Pennac**

There is no education system in the world - none at all - that's better than its average teacher.
- David Puttnam

If a teacher does not involve himself, his values, his commitments, in the course of discussion, why should the students?
- Paul Wellstone

I could undertake to be an efficient pupil if it were possible to find an efficient teacher.
- Gertrude Stein

There is no recipe to be a great teacher, that's what is unique about them.
- Robert Sternberg

Think of your favorite teacher you ever had in school: the one who made it the most fun to go to class. They surprise you. They keep you guessing. They keep you coming back, wanting to know what's going to happen next.
- Pete Carroll

A teacher enlarges people in all sorts of ways besides just his subject matter.
- **Wallace Stegner**

It is not easy to imagine how little interested a scientist usually is in the work of any other, with the possible exception of the teacher who backs him or the student who honors him.
- **Jean Rostand**

In other words, if a teacher only teaches in one way, then they conclude that the kids who can't learn well that way don't have the ability, when, in fact, it may be that the way the teacher's teaching is not a particularly good match to the way those kids learn.
- **Robert Sternberg**

There's no question that a great teacher can make a huge difference in a student's achievement, and we need to recruit, train and reward more such teachers. But here's what some new studies are also showing: We need better parents. Parents more focused on their children's education can also make a huge difference in a student's achievement.
- **Thomas Friedman**

Without any doubt at all, teacher quality is the fundamental differentiator. Not just, incidentally, of education, but I would argue, probably the biggest single differentiator of success for the nations of the 21st Century.

- David Puttnam

As a teacher you are more or less obliged to pay the same amount of attention to everything. That can wear you down.

- Marilyn Hacker

As a teacher, my strategy is to encourage questioning. I'm the least authoritarian professor you'll ever meet.

- Niall Ferguson

Ensuring all kids have access to an effective, talented teacher needs to be a national priority.

- Michael Bennet

As places of learning, schools have a responsibility to also educate on nutrition, which we all can agree is far more important than algebra, no matter what your third-period teacher claims.

- Lynda Resnick

As a former high school teacher, I know that investing in education is one of the most important things we can do, not only for our children, but for the benefit of our whole community.
- **Ed Pastor**

I do think we know that a teacher who knows what he or she is doing, knows their subject matter, and knows how to impart knowledge to kids is a critical piece of closing the achievement gap.
- **Margaret Spellings**

A father is a person who's around, participating in a child's life. He's a teacher who helps to guide and shape and mold that young person, someone for that young person to talk to, to share with, their ups and their downs, their fears and their concerns.
- **Michael Nutter**

A great teacher who is full of excitement and love for her students can make all the difference in their lives.
- **Deval Patrick**

I believe there's not a harder job in the world than being a teacher, and there isn't a job with a more direct impact on the performance of our students.
- **Michael Bennet**

Every writing teacher gives the subliminal message, every time they teach: 'Your life counts for something.' In no other subject that I know of is that message given.
- Roger Rosenblatt

When students have thanked me in the past for being their teacher, I have always felt that it was actually my love for the art of teaching they were speaking to.
- Taylor Mali

It is commonly said that a teacher fails if he has not been surpassed by his students. There has been no failure on our part in this regard considering how far they have gone.
- Edmond H. Fischer

A wisely chosen illustration is almost essential to fasten the truth upon the ordinary mind, and no teacher can afford to neglect this part of his preparation.
- Howard Crosby

They say that people teach what they need to learn. By adopting the role of happiness teacher, if only for myself, I was trying to find the method to conquer my particular faults and limitations.
- Gretchen Rubin

We can not wait until we have enough trained people willing to work at a teacher's salary and under conditions imposed upon teachers in order to improve what happens in the classroom.

- Major Owens

The Chinese are brought up to believe that you should be silent in class. The teacher speaks, and you just listen and absorb what they say.

- Caleb Deschanel

Education

Education is the most powerful weapon, which you can use to change the world.
- **- Nelson Mandela**

The roots of education are bitter, but the fruit is sweet.
- **- Aristotle**

The function of education is to teach one to think intensively and to think critically. Intelligence plus character - that is the goal of true education.
- **- Martin Luther King, Jr.**

Education is the key to unlock the golden door of freedom.
- **- George Washington Carver**

Education is not preparation for life; education is life itself.
- **- John Dewey**

Education is the best friend. An educated person is respected everywhere. Education beats the beauty and the youth.
- **- Chanakya**

Education is the movement from darkness to light.
— **Allan Bloom**

An investment in knowledge pays the best interest.
— **Benjamin Franklin**

My mother said I must always be intolerant of ignorance but understanding of illiteracy. That some people, unable to go to school, were more educated and more intelligent than college professors.
— **Maya Angelou**

The only person who is educated is the one who has learned how to learn and change.
— **Carl Rogers**

You are always a student, never a master. You have to keep moving forward.
— **Conrad Hall**

The goal of education is the advancement of knowledge and the dissemination of truth.
— **John F. Kennedy**

Education is learning what you didn't even know you didn't know.
- **Daniel J. Boorstin**

Education is an admirable thing, but it is well to remember from time to time that nothing that is worth knowing can be taught.
- **Oscar Wilde**

The most influential of all educational factors is the conversation in a child's home.
- **William Temple**

He who opens a school door, closes a prison.
- **Victor Hugo**

Education is not the filling of a pail, but the lighting of a fire.
- **William Butler Yeats**

Any man who reads too much and uses his own brain too little falls into lazy habits of thinking.
- **Albert Einstein**

The illiterate of the future will not be the person who cannot read. It will be the person who does not know how to learn.
- Alvin Toffler

No one has yet realized the wealth of sympathy, the kindness and generosity hidden in the soul of a child. The effort of every true education should be to unlock that treasure.
- Emma Goldman

A human being is not attaining his full heights until he is educated.
- Horace Mann

The object of education is to prepare the young to educate themselves throughout their lives.
- Robert M. Hutchins

Your library is your paradise.
- Desiderius Erasmus

It is a miracle that curiosity survives formal education.
- Albert Einstein

Education is all a matter of building bridges.
- Ralph Ellison

Much education today is monumentally ineffective. All too often we are giving young people cut flowers when we should be teaching them to grow their own plants.
- John W. Gardner

He that loves reading has everything within his reach.
- William Godwin

Learning is not attained by chance; it must be sought for with ardor and diligence.
- Abigail Adams

The purpose of education is to replace an empty mind with an open one.
- Malcolm Forbes

Develop a passion for learning. If you do, you will never cease to grow.
- Anthony J. D'Angelo

To educate a man in mind and not in morals is to educate a menace to society.
- Theodore Roosevelt

If I were again beginning my studies, I would follow the advice of Plato and start with mathematics.
- Galileo Galilei

The foundation of every state is the education of its youth.
- Diogenes

Don't limit a child to your own learning, for he was born in another time.
- Rabindranath Tagore

A library is the delivery room for the birth of ideas, a place where history comes to life.
- Norman Cousins

I would rather entertain and hope that people learned something than educate people and hope they were entertained.
- Walt Disney

An education isn't how much you have committed to memory, or even how much you know. It's being able to differentiate between what you know and what you don't.
- Anatole France

Poor people cannot rely on the government to come to help you in times of need. You have to get your education. Then nobody can control your destiny.
- Charles Barkley

Data is not information, information is not knowledge, knowledge is not understanding, understanding is not wisdom.
- Clifford Stoll

Education is a progressive discovery of our own ignorance.
- Will Durant

Good questions outrank easy answers.
- Paul Samuelson

What sculpture is to a block of marble, education is to the soul.
- Joseph Addison

The only thing that interferes with my learning is my education.

- Albert Einstein

Intellectual growth should commence at birth and cease only at death.

- Albert Einstein

Education is what survives when what has been learned has been forgotten.

- B. F. Skinner

Good teaching is one-fourth preparation and three-fourths pure theatre.

- Gail Godwin

Change is the end result of all true learning.

- Leo Buscaglia

Men and women must be educated, in a great degree, by the opinions and manners of the society they live in.

- Mary Wollstonecraft

It is a thousand times better to have common sense without education than to have education without common sense.
— **Robert Green Ingersoll**

Nine tenths of education is encouragement.
— **Anatole France**

To read without reflecting is like eating without digesting.
— **Edmund Burke**

The great aim of education is not knowledge but action.
— **Herbert Spencer**

Children have to be educated, but they have also to be left to educate themselves.
— **Ernest Dimnet**

Some people will never learn anything, for this reason, because they understand everything too soon.
— **Alexander Pope**

Rewards and punishments are the lowest form of education.
— **Zhuangzi**

Why should society feel responsible only for the education of children, and not for the education of all adults of every age?
> **- Erich Fromm**

Education... has produced a vast population able to read but unable to distinguish what is worth reading.
> **- G. M. Trevelyan**

The simplest schoolboy is now familiar with truths for which Archimedes would have sacrificed his life.
> **- Ernest Renan**

When I get a little money I buy books; and if any is left I buy food and clothes.
> **- Desiderius Erasmus**

Man is what he reads.
> **- Joseph Brodsky**

The only real failure in life is one not learned from.
> **- Anthony J. D'Angelo**

I am sure my fellow-scientists will agree with me if I say that whatever we were able to achieve in our later years had its origin in the experiences of our youth and in the hopes and wishes which were formed before and during our time as students.

- Felix Bloch

The great difficulty in education is to get experience out of ideas.

- George Santayana

True, a little learning is a dangerous thing, but it still beats total ignorance.

- Pauline Phillips

Academic qualifications are important and so is financial education. They're both important and schools are forgetting one of them.

- Robert Kiyosaki

While there are many obstacles that deter students from going to college, finances by no means should be the deciding factor.

- Bobby Scott

He who studies books alone will know how things ought to be, and he who studies men will know how they are.

- Charles Caleb Colton

Education is the key to success in life, and teachers make a lasting impact in the lives of their students.

- Solomon Ortiz

Education is the passport to the future, for tomorrow belongs to those who prepare for it today.

- Malcolm X

Nothing in this world can take the place of persistence. Talent will not: nothing is more common than unsuccessful men with talent. Genius will not; unrewarded genius is almost a proverb. Education will not: the world is full of educated derelicts. Persistence and determination alone are omnipotent.

- Calvin Coolidge

Knowledge is power. Information is liberating. Education is the premise of progress, in every society, in every family.

- Kofi Annan

Education, n.: That which discloses to the wise and disguises from the foolish their lack of understanding.
— **Ambrose Bierce**

Formal education will make you a living; self-education will make you a fortune.
— **Jim Rohn**

Education is the key to the future: You've heard it a million times, and it's not wrong. Educated people have higher wages and lower unemployment rates, and better-educated countries grow faster and innovate more than other countries. But going to college is not enough. You also have to study the right subjects.
— **Alex Tabarrok**

Education begins the gentleman, but reading, good company and reflection must finish him.
— **John Locke**

Research shows that there is only half as much variation in student achievement between schools as there is among classrooms in the same school. If you want your child to get the best education possible, it is actually more important to get him assigned to a great teacher than to a great school.
— **Bill Gates**

Without education, your children can never really meet the challenges they will face. So it's very important to give children education and explain that they should play a role for their country.
- Nelson Mandela

In some parts of the world, students are going to school every day. It's their normal life. But in other part of the world, we are starving for education... it's like a precious gift. It's like a diamond.
- Malala Yousafzai

Education is that whole system of human training within and without the schoolhouse walls, which molds and develops men.
- W. E. B. Du Bois

The aim of education is the knowledge, not of facts, but of values.
- William S. Burroughs

Education is a weapon whose effects depend on who holds it in his hands and at whom it is aimed.
- Joseph Stalin

Education is a shared commitment between dedicated teachers, motivated students and enthusiastic parents with high expectations.

- Bob Beauprez

The principle goal of education in the schools should be creating men and women who are capable of doing new things, not simply repeating what other generations have done.

- Jean Piaget

Democracy cannot succeed unless those who express their choice are prepared to choose wisely. The real safeguard of democracy, therefore, is education.

- Franklin D. Roosevelt

There is no end to education. It is not that you read a book, pass an examination, and finish with education. The whole of life, from the moment you are born to the moment you die, is a process of learning.

- Jiddu Krishnamurti

To succeed, you will soon learn, as I did, the importance of a solid foundation in the basics of education - literacy, both verbal and numerical, and communication skills.

- Alan Greenspan

We discovered that education is not something which the teacher does, but that it is a natural process which develops spontaneously in the human being.
- **Maria Montessori**

The greatest education in the world is watching the masters at work.
- **Michael Jackson**

If you think education is expensive, try ignorance.
- **Derek Bok**

There is no greater education than one that is self-driven.
- **Neil deGrasse Tyson**

All I want is an education, and I am afraid of no one.
- **Malala Yousafzai**

Our future growth relies on competitiveness and innovation, skills and productivity... and these in turn rely on the education of our people.
- **Julia Gillard**

There are many problems, but I think there is a solution to all these problems; it's just one, and it's education.
- Malala Yousafzai

Good manners will open doors that the best education cannot.
- Clarence Thomas

Education without values, as useful as it is, seems rather to make man a more clever devil.
- C. S. Lewis

We have an obligation and a responsibility to be investing in our students and our schools. We must make sure that people who have the grades, the desire and the will, but not the money, can still get the best education possible.
- Barack Obama

If you want to get laid, go to college. If you want an education, go to the library.
- **Frank Zappa**

Real education should consist of drawing the goodness and the best out of our own students. What better books can there be than the book of humanity?
- **Cesar Chavez**

The mere imparting of information is not education.
- **Carter G. Woodson**

The education of a man is never completed until he dies.
- **Robert E. Lee**

Do you know the difference between education and experience? Education is when you read the fine print; experience is what you get when you don't.
- **Pete Seeger**

Without education, you are not going anywhere in this world.
- **Malcolm X**

Education is for improving the lives of others and for leaving your community and world better than you found it.
- **Marian Wright Edelman**

There is no greater education than one that is self-driven.
- Neil deGrasse Tyson

Instead of a national curriculum for education, what is really needed is an individual curriculum for every child.
- Charles Handy

Education is not only a ladder of opportunity, but it is also an investment in our future.
- Ed Markey

Education is a human right with immense power to transform. On its foundation rest the cornerstones of freedom, democracy and sustainable human development.
- Kofi Annan

I believed in studying just because I knew education was a privilege. It was the discipline of study, to get into the habit of doing something that you don't want to do.
- Wynton Marsalis

Anyone who tries to make a distinction between education and entertainment doesn't know the first thing about either.
- Marshall McLuhan

Don't let schooling interfere with your education.
— **Mark Twain**

Traditional education is based on facts and figures and passing tests - not on a comprehension of the material and its application to your life.
— **Will Smith**

I had a terrible education. I attended a school for emotionally disturbed teachers.
— **Woody Allen**

True education is concerned not only with practical goals but also with values. Our aims assure us of our material life, our values make possible our spiritual life.
— **Ludwig Mies van der Rohe**

I think that probably the most important thing about our education was that it taught us to question even those things we thought we knew. To say you've got to inquire, you've got to be testing your knowledge all the time in order to be more effective in what you're doing.
— **Thabo Mbeki**

I believe that education is all about being excited about something. Seeing passion and enthusiasm helps push an educational message.

— **Steve Irwin**

Ensuring quality higher education is one of the most important things we can do for future generations.

— **Ron Lewis**

I wish I had known that education is the key. That knowledge is power. Now I pick up books and watch educational shows with my husband. I'm seeing how knowledge can elevate you.

— **Mary J. Blige**

Cauliflower is nothing but cabbage with a college education.

— **Mark Twain**

Next in importance to freedom and justice is popular education, without which neither freedom nor justice can be permanently maintained.

— **James A. Garfield**

When you have a problem, rules don't solve your problem. It's caring and education.
- **Jim Brown**

The progress of the world depends almost entirely upon education.
- **George Eastman**

Reformation, like education, is a journey, not a destination.
- **Mary Harris Jones**

I also tell them that your education can take you way farther than a football, baseball, track, or basketball will - that's just the bottom line.
- **Bo Jackson**

It makes little difference how many university courses or degrees a person may own. If he cannot use words to move an idea from one point to another, his education is incomplete.
- **Norman Cousins**

The most important part of education is proper training in the nursery.
- **Plato**

I am a firm believer that upon release, ex-offenders should be afforded a second chance to become productive citizens by providing rehabilitation and education that will help them join the workforce.

- **Charles B. Rangel**

I have always had this view about the modern education system: we pay attention to brain development, but the development of warm-heartedness we take for granted.

- **Dalai Lama**

Our school education ignores, in a thousand ways, the rules of healthy development.

- **Elizabeth Blackwell**

In the new economy, information, education, and motivation are everything.

- **William J. Clinton**

Steve Jobs, Bill Gates and Mark Zuckerberg didn't finish college. Too much emphasis is placed on formal education - I told my children not to worry about their grades but to enjoy learning.

- **Nassim Nicholas Taleb**

We are faced with the paradoxical fact that education has become one of the chief obstacles to intelligence and freedom of thought.
- **Bertrand Russell**

America believes in education: the average professor earns more money in a year than a professional athlete earns in a whole week.
- **Evan Esar**

Good education is so important. We do need to look at the way people are taught. It not just about qualifications to get a job. It's about being educated.
- **Zaha Hadid**

I tell students that the opportunities I had were a result of having a good educational background. Education is what allows you to stand out.
- **Ellen Ochoa**

The giving of love is an education in itself.
- **Eleanor Roosevelt**

When you go somewhere like Kenya and you see how the children don't have pencils and pens, and all of these things are considered luxuries, and what a privilege they see education as and how hungry they are to learn, I wanted to give my brother and sister long lectures. That definitely stayed with me.

- Naomie Harris

In our education system, we are taught to munch figures and remember them for lifetime. But does it help? We are not taught how to make decisions.

- Chetan Bhagat

Education promotes equality and lifts people out of poverty. It teaches children how to become good citizens. Education is not just for a privileged few, it is for everyone. It is a fundamental human right.

- Ban Ki-moon

Crucial to science education is hands-on involvement: showing, not just telling; real experiments and field trips and not just 'virtual reality.'

- Martin Rees

Education is the best provision for old age.

- Aristotle

Everyone who remembers his own education remembers teachers, not methods and techniques. The teacher is the heart of the educational system.

- Sidney Hook

As a high school dropout, I understand the value of education: A second chance at obtaining my high school diploma through the G.I. Bill led me to attend college and law school and allowed me the opportunity to serve in Congress.

- Charles B. Rangel

Education in our times must try to find whatever there is in students that might yearn for completion, and to reconstruct the learning that would enable them autonomously to seek that completion.

- Allan Bloom

It's not enough to train today's workforce. We also have to prepare tomorrow's workforce by guaranteeing every child access to a world-class education.

- Barack Obama

The answer is not to standardize education, but to personalize and customize it to the needs of each child and community. There is no alternative. There never was.

- Sir Ken Robinson

Our progress as a nation can be no swifter than our progress in education. The human mind is our fundamental resource.
- John F. Kennedy

Education is a continual process; it's like a bicycle... If you don't pedal you don't go forward.
- George Weah

No other investment yields as great a return as the investment in education. An educated workforce is the foundation of every community and the future of every economy.
- Brad Henry

If a man neglects education, he walks lame to the end of his life.
- Plato

You may be a redneck if... you have spent more on your pickup truck than on your education.
- Jeff Foxworthy

Men are born ignorant, not stupid. They are made stupid by education.

- Bertrand Russell

Education is not merely neglected in many of our schools today, but is replaced to a great extent by ideological indoctrination.

- Thomas Sowell

One of the most powerful tools for empowering individuals and communities is making certain that any individual who wants to receive a quality education can do so.

- Christine Gregoire

Self-education is, I firmly believe, the only kind of education there is.

- Isaac Asimov

Genius without education is like silver in the mine.

- Benjamin Franklin

If education does not create a need for the best in life, then we are stuck in an undemocratic, rigid caste society.

- Sargent Shriver

Economists who have studied the relationship between education and economic growth confirm what common sense suggests: The number of college degrees is not nearly as important as how well students develop cognitive skills, such as critical thinking and problem-solving ability.
- Derek Bok

Natural ability without education has more often raised a man to glory and virtue than education without natural ability.
- Marcus Aurelius

When you have a father and a mother who work all their lives so you can have an education and build your body - it's a blessing.
- Lou Gehrig

The true purpose of education is to teach a man to carry himself triumphant to the sunset.
- Liberty Hyde Bailey

Education is the investment our generation makes in the future.
- Mitt Romney

It might be said now that I have the best of both worlds. A Harvard education and a Yale degree.
- **John F. Kennedy**

Education is not to reform students or amuse them or to make them expert technicians. It is to unsettle their minds, widen their horizons, inflame their intellects, teach them to think straight, if possible.
- **Robert M. Hutchins**

A quality education grants us the ability to fight the war on ignorance and poverty.
- **Charles B. Rangel**

Without education we are in a horrible and deadly danger of taking educated people seriously.
- **Gilbert K. Chesterton**

When a person is humiliated, when his rights are being violated, and he does not have the proper education, naturally he gravitates toward terrorism.
- **Shirin Ebadi**

How is it that little children are so intelligent and men so stupid? It must be education that does it.
- Alexandre Dumas

If you improve education by teaching for competence, eliminating schooling, and connecting with students, the test scores will improve.
- William Glasser

We need another revolution in the Arab world. We need an education revolution. If there's one thing we need to focus on, it's redesigning our educational systems.
- Queen Rania of Jordan

A good education gives you confidence to stick up your hand for anything - whether it is the job you want, or the bloke. And the more you stick up your hand, the better your chances are that you will get what you want.
- Kate Reardon

Education is everything - education is your power, education is your way in life for whatever you want to do.
- Ciara

Ever since economists revealed how much universities contribute to economic growth, politicians have paid close attention to higher education.

- Derek Bok

Education must begin with the solution of the student-teacher contradiction, by reconciling the poles of the contradiction so that both are simultaneously teachers and students.

- Paulo Freire

Through books and photographs, I saw a world that was not my own - and I realized that there was another world. That's why I'm concerned about education, because it helps our children see other worlds.

- Bette Midler

By providing students in our Nation with such an education, we help save our children from the clutches of poverty, crime, drugs, and hopelessness, and we help safeguard our Nation's prosperity for generations yet unborn.

- Elijah Cummings

Education exposes young people to a broader world, a world full of opportunity and hope.

- Christine Gregoire

The arts, sciences, humanities, physical education, languages and maths all have equal and central contributions to make to a student's education.
- Sir Ken Robinson

If someone is going down the wrong road, he doesn't need motivation to speed him up. What he needs is education to turn him around.
- Jim Rohn

Education is not just about going to school and getting a degree. It's about widening your knowledge and absorbing the truth about life.
- Shakuntala Devi

Our youth deserve the opportunity to complete their high school and college education, free of early parenthood. Their future children deserve the opportunity to grow up in financially and emotionally stable homes. Our communities benefit from healthy, productive, well-prepared young people.
- Jane Fonda

Education must, be not only a transmission of culture but also a provider of alternative views of the world and a strengthener of the will to explore them.
- Jerome Bruner

This is at the heart of all good education, where the teacher asks students to think and engages them in encouraging dialogues, constantly checking for understanding and growth.

- William Glasser

Vocational education programs have made a real difference in the lives of countless young people nationwide; they build self-confidence and leadership skills by allowing students to utilize their unique gifts and talents.

- Conrad Burns

Apply yourself. Get all the education you can, but then, by God, do something. Don't just stand there, make it happen.

- Lee Iacocca

I will get my education - if it is in home, school, or anyplace.

- Malala Yousafzai

Education is freedom.

- Paulo Freire

Human history becomes more and more a race between education and catastrophe.
- H. G. Wells

Education is not merely neglected in many of our schools today, but is replaced to a great extent by ideological indoctrination.
- Thomas Sowell

Prejudices, it is well known, are most difficult to eradicate from the heart whose soil has never been loosened or fertilized by education; they grow firm there, firm as weeds among stones.
- Charlotte Bronte

There is no education like adversity.
- Benjamin Disraeli

There are over 200 million illiterate women in India. This low literacy negatively impacts not just their lives but also their families' and the country's economic development. A girl's lack of education also has a negative impact on the health and well-being of her children.
- Sachin Tendulkar

Good education means learning to read, write and most importantly learn how to learn so that you can be whatever you want to be when you grow up.

- Patty Murray

Every kid, every minority kid can be so successful if they focus on their education.

- Magic Johnson

Liberating education consists in acts of cognition, not transferrals of information.

- Paulo Freire

Looking back, I realize that nurturing curiosity and the instinct to seek solutions are perhaps the most important contributions education can make.

- Paul Berg

The dream doesn't lie in victimization or blame; it lies in hard work, determination and a good education.

- Alphonso Jackson

Real education should educate us out of self into something far finer; into a selflessness which links us with all humanity.

- Nancy Astor

The most valuable of all education is the ability to make yourself do the thing you have to do, when it has to be done, whether you like it or not.

- Aldous Huxley

Education comes from within; you get it by struggle and effort and thought.

- Napoleon Hill

We have entered an age in which education is not just a luxury permitting some men an advantage over others. It has become a necessity without which a person is defenseless in this complex, industrialized society. We have truly entered the century of the educated man.

- Lyndon B. Johnson

If you want to thrive in today's economy, you must challenge the status quo and get the financial education necessary to succeed.

- Robert Kiyosaki

I think an education is not only important, it is the most important thing you can do with your life.
- Dean Kamen

Inclusive, good-quality education is a foundation for dynamic and equitable societies.
- Desmond Tutu

All men who have turned out worth anything have had the chief hand in their own education.
- Walter Scott

Education is important because, first of all, people need to know that discrimination still exists. It is still real in the workplace, and we should not take that for granted.
- Alexis Herman

To accuse others for one's own misfortunes is a sign of want of education. To accuse oneself shows that one's education has begun. To accuse neither oneself nor others shows that one's education is complete.
- Epictetus

The goal of higher education should be to champion the airing of all honest viewpoints. Nothing less is acceptable.
- Bill O'Reilly

Widespread public access to knowledge, like public education, is one of the pillars of our democracy, a guarantee that we can maintain a well-informed citizenry.
- Scott Turow

To throw obstacles in the way of a complete education is like putting out the eyes.
- Elizabeth Cady Stanton

I never got a formal education. So my intellect is my common sense. I don't have anything else going for me. And my common sense opens the door to instinct.
- Jerry Lewis

We pay a price when we deprive children of the exposure to the values, principles, and education they need to make them good citizens.
- Sandra Day O'Connor

A good education is another name for happiness.
- Ann Plato

Education comes from within; you get it by struggle and effort and thought.
- Napoleon Hill

Nothing in education is so astonishing as the amount of ignorance it accumulates in the form of inert facts.
- Henry Adams

There is no cost difference between incarceration and an Ivy League education; the main difference is curriculum.
- Paul Hawken

In the long run, your human capital is your main base of competition. Your leading indicator of where you're going to be 20 years from now is how well you're doing in your education system.
- Bill Gates

You know, nothing is more important than education, because nowhere are our stakes higher; our future depends on the quality of education of our children today.
- Arnold Schwarzenegger

Let's not leave an educational vacuum to be filled by religious extremists who go to families who have no other option and offer meals, housing and some form of education. If we are going to combat extremism then we must educate those very same children.

- Hillary Clinton

I don't think anybody anywhere can talk about the future of their people or of an organization without talking about education. Whoever controls the education of our children controls our future.

- Wilma Mankiller

No one can get an education, for of necessity education is a continuing process.

- Louis L'Amour

The education of women is the best way to save the environment.

- E. O. Wilson

Education is not a problem. Education is an opportunity.

- Lyndon B. Johnson

The aim of education is the knowledge not of facts but of values.

- William Ralph Inge

Education must provide the opportunities for self-fulfilment; it can at best provide a rich and challenging environment for the individual to explore, in his own way.

- Noam Chomsky

The ultimate goal of the educational system is to shift to the individual the burden of pursing his own education. This will not be a widely shared pursuit until we get over our odd conviction that education is what goes on in school buildings and nowhere else.

- John W. Gardner

Education commences at the mother's knee, and every word spoken within hearsay of little children tends toward the formation of character.

- Hosea Ballou

You have to go through the falling down in order to learn to walk. It helps to know that you can survive it. That's an education in itself.

- Carol Burnett

In a way, education by its nature favours the extrovert because you are taking kids and putting them into a big classroom, which is automatically going to be a high-stimulation environment. Probably the best way of teaching in general is one on one, but that's not something everyone can afford.

— **Susan Cain**

Access to books and the encouragement of the habit of reading: these two things are the first and most necessary steps in education and librarians, teachers and parents all over the country know it. It is our children's right and it is also our best hope and their best hope for the future.

— **Michael Morpurgo**

In these days, it is doubtful that any child may reasonably be expected to succeed in life if he is denied the opportunity of an education.

— **Earl Warren**

Education is the best economic policy there is.

— **Tony Blair**

To live for a time close to great minds is the best kind of education.

— **John Buchan**

A good education is that which prepares us for our future sphere of action and makes us contented with that situation in life in which God, in his infinite mercy, has seen fit to place us, to be perfectly resigned to our lot in life, whatever it may be.
- Ann Plato

Education, like neurosis, begins at home.
- Milton Sapirstein

The best education in the world is that got by struggling to get a living.
- Wendell Phillips

Education exposes young people to a broader world, a world full of opportunity and hope.
- Christine Gregoire

Although children are only 24 percent of the population, they're 100 percent of our future and we cannot afford to provide any child with a substandard education.
- Ed Markey

Let us not, in the eagerness of our haste to educate, forget all the ends of education.

- William Godwin

Of all the public services, education is the one I'm most interested in. You get a more dynamic economy, you deal with most social problems, and it's morally right.

- George Osborne

Most Indians go into education. Their parents just push them into education like parents in Australia push them into sports.

- Mahesh Bhupathi

Both class and race survive education, and neither should. What is education then? If it doesn't help a human being to recognize that humanity is humanity, what is it for? So you can make a bigger salary than other people?

- Beah Richards

When you revolutionize education, you're taking the very mechanism of how people can be smarter and do new things, and you're priming the pump for so many incredible things.

- Bill Gates

Too much of what is called 'education' is little more than an expensive isolation from reality.

- Thomas Sowell

No group and no government can properly prescribe precisely what should constitute the body of knowledge with which true education is concerned.

- Franklin D. Roosevelt

If we want boys to succeed, we need to bring them back to education by making education relevant to them and bring in more service learning and vocational education.

- Michael Gurian

Education is not a tool for development - individual, community and the nation. It is the foundation for our future. It is empowerment to make choices and emboldens the youth to chase their dreams.

- Nita Ambani

You can't legislate good will - that comes through education.

- Malcolm X

Nature has always had more force than education.
— **Voltaire**

Education is the cheap defense of nations.
— **Edmund Burke**

Common sense is in spite of, not as the result of education.
— **Victor Hugo**

Universal education is not only a moral imperative but an economic necessity, to pave the way toward making many more nations self-sufficient and self-sustaining.
— **Desmond Tutu**

Upon the education of the people of this country the fate of this country depends.
— **Benjamin Disraeli**

I know what it feels like to struggle to get the education that you need.
— **Michelle Obama**

Education begins at home and I applaud the parents who recognize that they - not someone else - must take responsibility to assure that their children are well educated.
- Ernest Istook

All claims of education notwithstanding, the pupil will accept only that which his mind craves.
- Emma Goldman

Education forms the common mind. Just as the twig is bent, the tree's inclined.
- Alexander Pope

The child who desires education will be bettered by it; the child who dislikes it disgraced.
- John Ruskin

I do sometimes accuse people of ignorance, but that is not intended to be an insult. I'm ignorant of lots of things. Ignorance is something that can be remedied by education.
- Richard Dawkins

Education is the period during which you are being instructed by somebody you do not know, about something you do not want to know.
— **Gilbert K. Chesterton**

An education which does not cultivate the will is an education that depraves the mind.
— **Anatole France**

Until we have comprehensive financial education, we'll never see the end of our booms and busts.
— **Robert Kiyosaki**

Education begins at home. You can't blame the school for not putting into your child what you don't put into him.
— **Geoffrey Holder**

Sixty years ago I knew everything; now I know nothing; education is a progressive discovery of our own ignorance.
— **Will Durant**

Television could perform a great service in mass education, but there's no indication its sponsors have anything like this on their minds.
— **Tallulah Bankhead**

Every single major push in education has made it worse and right now it's really bad because everything we've done is de-humanizing education. It's destroying the possibility of the teacher and the student having a warm, friendly, intellectual relationship.
- William Glasser

A wise system of education will at last teach us how little man yet knows, how much he has still to learn.
- John Lubbock

The supreme lesson of any education should be to think for yourself and to be yourself; absent this attainment, education creates dangerous, stupefying conformity.
- Bryant H. McGill

The main part of intellectual education is not the acquisition of facts, but learning how to make facts live.
- Oliver Wendell Holmes, Jr.

One of my great laments is that education today seems to have... be less about passion and more about process, more about tactic or technique.
- Neil deGrasse Tyson

But I look at failure as education. In that respect, I am so well-educated.

Kathy Ireland

Education is a crutch with which the foolish attack the wise to prove that they are not idiots.

- Karl Kraus

For me, I was somebody who was a smart young guy who didn't do very well in school. The basic system of education, I didn't fit in; my intelligence was elsewhere.

- Bruce Springsteen

What is defeat? Nothing but education. Nothing but the first step to something better.

- Wendell Phillips

To defend a country you need an army, but to defend a civilization you need education.

- Jonathan Sacks

The length of your education is less important than its breadth, and the length of your life is less important than its depth.

- Marilyn vos Savant

Education, whatever else it should or should not be, must be an inoculation against the poisons of life and an adequate equipment in knowledge and skill for meeting the chances of life.

- Havelock Ellis

Just think of the opportunities we can unlock by making education as addictive as a video game. This type of experiential, addictive learning improves decision-making skills and increases the processing speed and spatial skills of the brain. When was the last time your child asked for help with a video game?

- Naveen Jain

My father is a real idealist, and he's all about learning. If I asked for a pair of Nikes growing up, it was just a resounding 'No.' But if I asked for a saxophone, one would appear and next day and I'd be signed up for lessons. So anything to do with education or learning, my father would spare no expense.

Hugh Jackman

True education flowers at the point when delight falls in love with responsibility.

- Philip Pullman

To live for a time close to great minds is the best kind of education.
- **John Buchan**

Strange as it may seem, no amount of learning can cure stupidity, and formal education positively fortifies it.
- **Stephen Vizinczey**

One of the great failings of our education system is that we tend to focus on those who are succeeding in exams, and there are plenty of them. But what we should also be looking at, and a lot more urgently, is those who fail.
- **Michael Morpurgo**

The best education I have ever received was through travel.
- **Lisa Ling**

It is as impossible to withhold education from the receptive mind, as it is impossible to force it upon the unreasoning.
- **Agnes Repplier**

Education is the mother of leadership.
- **Wendell Willkie**

Likewise, education can direct people toward good or evil ends. When education is based on a fundamentally distorted worldview, the results are horrific.
- **Daisaku Ikeda**

If we had in this room a hundred teachers, good teachers from good schools, and asked them to define the word education, there would be very little general agreement.
- **William Glasser**

Economic prosperity and quality education for our children are inexorably linked.
- **Jon Huntsman, Jr.**

Early childhood education begins early, even before birth.
- **Madeleine M. Kunin**

Learning starts with failure; the first failure is the beginning of education.
- **John Hersey**

The great end of education is to discipline rather than to furnish the mind; to train it to the use of its own powers, rather than fill it with the accumulation of others.
- **Tryon Edwards**

When the state or federal government control the education of all of our children, they have the dangerous and illegitimate monopoly to control and influence the thought process of our citizens.
- Michael Badnarik

Every city across the country that has successfully renewed and revitalized itself points to a robust education system as its fundamental key to success.
- Alan Autry

Education is the only billion-dollar industry that tolerates abject failure.
- Geoffrey Canada

Civic education and civic responsibility should be taught in elementary school.
- Donna Brazile

Promoting education is an effort that is close to my heart. Illiteracy contributes to poverty; encouraging children to pick up a book is fundamental.
- Sasha Grey

As the true object of education is not to render the pupil the mere copy of his preceptor, it is rather to be rejoiced in, than lamented, that various reading should lead him into new trains of thinking.

- William Godwin

It is part of the work of education to have substantive relationships with your students.

- Freeman A. Hrabowski III

Ignorance and a narrow education lay the foundation of vice, and imitation and custom rear it up.

- Mary Astell

If we want our children to value education, then we must show our appreciation for knowledge.

- Brad Sherman

Martial arts should be part of every girl's education.

- Esha Gupta

I just thank my father and mother, my lucky stars, that I had the advantage of an education in the humanities.

- David McCullough

If we expect our children to thrive at our colleges and universities, and succeed in our economy once they graduate - first we must make quality, affordable early childhood education accessible to all.

- Kirsten Gillibrand

Knowledge is not just the preserve of the educated elite. Just because someone has not had a formal education, that does not mean he does not have wisdom and common sense.

- Vikas Swarup

An education program is, by definition, a societal program. Work should be done at school, rather than at home.

- Francois Hollande

From an early age I was told that I was expected to do more than continue to run a small business. Education was important and seen as a way of moving forward.

- John Pople

Being incarcerated is truly very serious, and it has changed my life to such an extent that breaking the cycle has become my sole focus. Jail is definitely not cool. Education is.

- Ja Rule

The gap in education in this country, the unfairness of the schools, is one of the great unfairness in this society.
- **Gaston Caperton**

If students get a sound education in the history, social effects and psychological biases of technology, they may grow to be adults who use technology rather than be used by it.
- **Neil Postman**

A lot of children, like I did, move away from words because of the fear - which is something you have to take out of education: the fear of worrying about what marks you'll get, detention, worrying about letting people down, your parents, teachers.
- **Michael Morpurgo**

Education is the transmission of civilization.
- **Ariel Durant**

An extended school day gives administrators the ability to ensure children get a well-rounded education.
- **Geoffrey Canada**

We have lots of evidence that putting investments in early childhood education, even evidence from very hard-nosed economists, is one of the very best investments that the society can possibly make. And yet we still don't have public support for things like preschools.

- Alison Gopnik

Here once again education is crucial, it enables children to be become more aware of their rights and to exercise them in a respectful manner which helps them shape their own future.

- Carol Bellamy

It was a slow understanding that the lack of education in a country like Somalia creates these huge social problems.

- Amanda Lindhout

By providing students in our Nation with such an education, we help save our children from the clutches of poverty, crime, drugs, and hopelessness, and we help safeguard our Nation's prosperity for generations yet unborn.

- Elijah Cummings

The want of education and moral training is the only real barrier that exists between the different classes of men.

- Susanna Moodie

Education helps you to be a well-rounded person, period. It teaches you how to take in information and data, process it, and use it for life building. Education was key in my family. You were going to college.
- **Yolanda Adams**

The great doctors all got their education off dirt pavements and poverty - not marble floors and foundations.
- **Martin H. Fischer**

Education is not a tool for development - individual, community and the nation. It is the foundation for our future. It is empowerment to make choices and emboldens the youth to chase their dreams.
- **Nita Ambani**

Our approach to education has remained largely unchanged since the Renaissance: From middle school through college, most teaching is done by an instructor lecturing to a room full of students, only some of them paying attention.
- **Daphne Koller**

Learning

Learning starts with failure; the first failure is the beginning of education.
- **John Hersey**

Tell me and I forget. Teach me and I remember. Involve me and I learn.
- **Benjamin Franklin**

You cannot open a book without learning something.
- **Confucius**

The ultimate lesson all of us have to learn is unconditional love, which includes not only others but ourselves as well.
- **Elisabeth Kubler-Ross**

You don't learn to walk by following rules. You learn by doing, and by falling over.
- **Richard Branson**

In youth we learn; in age we understand.
- **Marie von Ebner-Eschenbach**

Learning never exhausts the mind.
— **Leonardo da Vinci**

There is no end to education. It is not that you read a book, pass an examination, and finish with education. The whole of life, from the moment you are born to the moment you die, is a process of learning.
— **Jiddu Krishnamurti**

Education is what remains after one has forgotten what one has learned in school.
— **Albert Einstein**

I've learned that people will forget what you said, people will forget what you did, but people will never forget how you made them feel.
— **Maya Angelou**

Live as if you were to die tomorrow. Learn as if you were to live forever.
— **Mahatma Gandhi**

A wise man can learn more from a foolish question than a fool can learn from a wise answer.
— **Bruce Lee**

I never learned from a man who agreed with me.
- **Robert A. Heinlein**

I am always doing that which I cannot do, in order that I may learn how to do it.
- **Pablo Picasso**

We must learn to live together as brothers or perish together as fools.
- **Martin Luther King, Jr.**

He who learns but does not think, is lost! He who thinks but does not learn is in great danger.
- **Confucius**

Learn to get in touch with the silence within yourself, and know that everything in life has purpose. There are no mistakes, no coincidences, all events are blessings given to us to learn from.
- **Elisabeth Kubler-Ross**

I like to listen. I have learned a great deal from listening carefully. Most people never listen.
- **Ernest Hemingway**

The brighter you are, the more you have to learn.
— **- Don Herold**

What we face may look insurmountable. But I learned something from all those years of training and competing. I learned something from all those sets and reps when I didn't think I could lift another ounce of weight. What I learned is that we are always stronger than we know.
— **- Arnold Schwarzenegger**

I've learned that you shouldn't go through life with a catcher's mitt on both hands; you need to be able to throw something back.
— **- Maya Angelou**

The things that have been most valuable to me I did not learn in school.
— **- Will Smith**

I learned the value of hard work by working hard.
— **- Margaret Mead**

Your most unhappy customers are your greatest source of learning.
— **- Bill Gates**

To know oneself is to study oneself in action with another person.
- **Bruce Lee**

I am always ready to learn although I do not always like being taught.
- **Winston Churchill**

God lets everything happen for a reason. It's all a learning process, and you have to go from one level to another.
- **Mike Tyson**

A man only learns in two ways, one by reading, and the other by association with smarter people.
- **Will Rogers**

It is paradoxical that many educators and parents still differentiate between a time for learning and a time for play without seeing the vital connection between them.
- **Leo Buscaglia**

We should regret our mistakes and learn from them, but never carry them forward into the future with us.
- **Lucy Maud Montgomery**

We now accept the fact that learning is a lifelong process of keeping abreast of change. And the most pressing task is to teach people how to learn.

- Peter Drucker

I try to learn from the past, but I plan for the future by focusing exclusively on the present. That's where the fun is.

- Donald Trump

I have never met a man so ignorant that I couldn't learn something from him.

- Galileo Galilei

Losers live in the past. Winners learn from the past and enjoy working in the present toward the future.

- Denis Waitley

A single conversation across the table with a wise man is better than ten years mere study of books.

- Henry Wadsworth Longfellow

I am still learning.

- Michelangelo

It's what you learn after you know it all that counts.
- **John Wooden**

I never learn anything talking. I only learn things when I ask questions.
- **Lou Holtz**

It is not knowledge, but the act of learning, not possession but the act of getting there, which grants the greatest enjoyment.
- **Carl Friedrich Gauss**

In times of change learners inherit the earth; while the learned find themselves beautifully equipped to deal with a world that no longer exists.
- **Eric Hoffer**

I don't love studying. I hate studying. I like learning. Learning is beautiful.
- **Natalie Portman**

You teach best what you most need to learn.
- **Richard Bach**

The truth is that we can learn to condition our minds, bodies, and emotions to link pain or pleasure to whatever we choose. By changing what we link pain and pleasure to, we will instantly change our behaviors.

- Tony Robbins

Question everything. Learn something. Answer nothing.

- Euripides

I grow old learning something new every day.

- Solon

The minute that you're not learning I believe you're dead.

- Jack Nicholson

The hardest job kids face today is learning good manners without seeing any.

- Fred Astaire

The first problem for all of us, men and women, is not to learn, but to unlearn.

- Gloria Steinem

It is what we know already that often prevents us from learning.
— **Claude Bernard**

Being ignorant is not so much a shame, as being unwilling to learn.
— **Benjamin Franklin**

The trouble with learning from experience is that you never graduate.
— **Doug Larson**

Leadership and learning are indispensable to each other.
— **John F. Kennedy**

I made decisions that I regret, and I took them as learning experiences... I'm human, not perfect, like anybody else.
— **Queen Latifah**

Anyone who stops learning is old, whether at twenty or eighty. Anyone who keeps learning stays young. The greatest thing in life is to keep your mind young.
— **Henry Ford**

It has been said that 80% of what people learn is visual.
- Allen Klein

Change is the end result of all true learning.
- Leo Buscaglia

Winning is great, sure, but if you are really going to do something in life, the secret is learning how to lose. Nobody goes undefeated all the time. If you can pick up after a crushing defeat, and go on to win again, you are going to be a champion someday.
- Wilma Rudolph

Learning is the beginning of wealth. Learning is the beginning of health. Learning is the beginning of spirituality. Searching and learning is where the miracle process all begins.
- Jim Rohn

Learning and innovation go hand in hand. The arrogance of success is to think that what you did yesterday will be sufficient for tomorrow.
- William Pollard

Develop a passion for learning. If you do, you will never cease to grow.

— Anthony J. D'Angelo

Failure is a great teacher, and I think when you make mistakes and you recover from them and you treat them as valuable learning experiences, then you've got something to share.

— Steve Harvey

Learning is not attained by chance; it must be sought for with ardor and diligence.

— Abigail Adams

Play is often talked about as if it were a relief from serious learning. But for children play is serious learning. Play is really the work of childhood.

— Fred Rogers

Take those chances and you can achieve greatness, whereas if you go conservative, you'll never know. I truly believe what doesn't kill you makes you stronger. Even if you fail, learning and moving on is sometimes the best thing.

— Danica Patrick

Each life is made up of mistakes and learning, waiting and growing, practicing patience and being persistent.
> **- Billy Graham**

Learning is a result of listening, which in turn leads to even better listening and attentiveness to the other person. In other words, to learn from the child, we must have empathy, and empathy grows as we learn.
> **- Alice Miller**

The excitement of learning separates youth from old age. As long as you're learning you're not old.
> **- Rosalyn S. Yalow**

A good teacher must be able to put himself in the place of those who find learning hard.
> **- Eliphas Levi**

The important thing is to learn a lesson every time you lose. Life is a learning process and you have to try to learn what's best for you. Let me tell you, life is not fun when you're banging your head against a brick wall all the time.
> **- John McEnroe**

Success in management requires learning as fast as the world is changing.
- Warren Bennis

Poverty must not be a bar to learning and learning must offer an escape from poverty.
- Lyndon B. Johnson

Like success, failure is many things to many people. With Positive Mental Attitude, failure is a learning experience, a rung on the ladder, a plateau at which to get your thoughts in order and prepare to try again.
- W. Clement Stone

Life is like playing a violin solo in public and learning the instrument as one goes on.
- Samuel Butler

Don't limit a child to your own learning, for he was born in another time.
- Rabindranath Tagore

Learning happens in the minds and souls, not in the databases of multiple-choice tests.
- Sir Ken Robinson

I always say the minute I stop making mistakes is the minute I stop learning and I've definitely learned a lot.

- Miley Cyrus

Writing in a journal reminds you of your goals and of your learning in life. It offers a place where you can hold a deliberate, thoughtful conversation with yourself.

- Robin S. Sharma

My goal in the classroom was always to make sure they were having so much fun that they didn't realize they were learning.

- Rick Riordan

Be passionate and bold. Always keep learning. You stop doing useful things if you don't learn. So the last part to me is the key, especially if you have had some initial success. It becomes even more critical that you have the learning 'bit' always switched on.

- Satya Nadella

I saw as a teacher how, if you take that spark of learning that those children have, and you ignite it, you can take a child from any background to a lifetime of creativity and accomplishment.

- Paul Wellstone

Curiosity is the wick in the candle of learning.
- William Arthur Ward

The library is the temple of learning, and learning has liberated more people than all the wars in history.
- Carl T. Rowan

You never stop learning. If you have a teacher, you never stop being a student.
- Elisabeth Rohm

I'm passionate about learning. I'm passionate about life.
- Tom Cruise

Libraries allow children to ask questions about the world and find the answers. And the wonderful thing is that once a child learns to use a library, the doors to learning are always open.
- Laura Bush

We are all in the business of sales. Teachers sell students on learning, parents sell their children on making good grades and behaving, and traditional salesmen sell their products.
- Dave Ramsey

A child's learning is a function more of the characteristics of his classmates than those of the teacher.
- **James S. Coleman**

The highest activity a human being can attain is learning for understanding, because to understand is to be free.
- **Baruch Spinoza**

My advice to an aspiring actor would be to never stop learning or working for what you want. Nothing comes easy, ever, if you want something, you have to work for it. By working for it I mean work on your craft, learn from people who have something to teach. It's just like anything else, practice makes perfect.
- **James Lafferty**

Learning a foreign language, and the culture that goes with it, is one of the most useful things we can do to broaden the empathy and imaginative sympathy and cultural outlook of children.
- **Michael Gove**

In spite of discouragement and adversity, those who are happiest seem to have a way of learning from difficult times, becoming stronger, wiser and happier as a result.
- **Joseph B. Wirthlin**

The world is the true classroom. The most rewarding and important type of learning is through experience, seeing something with our own eyes.

- Jack Hanna

I have never forgotten my days as an Eagle Scout. I didn't know it at the time, but what really came out of my Scouting was learning how to lead and serve the community. It has come in handy in my career in government.

- Lloyd Bentsen

The most useful piece of learning for the uses of life is to unlearn what is untrue.

- Antisthenes

Responsibility for learning belongs to the student, regardless of age.

- Robert Martin

As long as I'm learning something, I figure I'm OK - it's a decent day.

- Hunter S. Thompson

I am learning all the time. The tombstone will be my diploma.
                                         - Eartha Kitt

Making a wrong decision is understandable. Refusing to search continually for learning is not.
                                         - Phil Crosby

The beautiful thing about learning is nobody can take it away from you.
                                         - B. B. King

Never become so much of an expert that you stop gaining expertise. View life as a continuous learning experience.
                                         - Denis Waitley

This life is a process of learning.
                                         - Lauryn Hill

Gardening is learning, learning, learning. That's the fun of them. You're always learning.
                                         - Helen Mirren

In the matter of learning, the difference between the earnest and the careless student stands out clearly. The same holds true in the mastering of passion and the weaknesses to which our nature is subject, as in the acquiring of virtue.

- Saint Ignatius

Why waste time learning, when ignorance is instantaneous?

- Bill Watterson

Life isn't about algebra and geometry. Learning by making mistakes and not duplicating them is what life is about.

- Lindsay Fox

I'm not going to school just for the academics - I wanted to share ideas, to be around people who are passionate about learning.

- Emma Watson

And I like asking questions, to keep learning; people with big egos might not want to look unsure.

- Heston Blumenthal

Much learning does not teach understanding.

- Heraclitus

Just because you are CEO, don't think you have landed. You must continually increase your learning, the way you think, and the way you approach the organization. I've never forgotten that.

- Indra Nooyi

Patience is a virtue, and I'm learning patience. It's a tough lesson.

- Elon Musk

Start with God - the first step in learning is bowing down to God; only fools thumb their noses at such wisdom and learning.

- King Solomon

I believe that the testing of the student's achievements in order to see if he meets some criterion held by the teacher, is directly contrary to the implications of therapy for significant learning.

- Carl Rogers

I am forever learning and changing.

- W. Edwards Deming

There's always failure. And there's always disappointment. And there's always loss. But the secret is learning from the loss, and realizing that none of those holes are vacuums.

- Michael J. Fox

There's no learning without trying lots of ideas and failing lots of times.

- Jonathan Ive

The process of learning requires not only hearing and applying but also forgetting and then remembering again.

- John Gray

You're always learning. The problem is, sometimes you stop and think you understand the world. This is not correct. The world is always moving. You never reach the point you can stop making an effort.

- Paulo Coelho

Neither comprehension nor learning can take place in an atmosphere of anxiety.

- Rose Kennedy

As long as you live, keep learning how to live.

- Lucius Annaeus Seneca

When you stop learning, stop listening, stop looking and asking questions, always new questions, then it is time to die.
- Lillian Smith

One of the reasons people stop learning is that they become less and less willing to risk failure.
- John W. Gardner

Never stop learning; knowledge doubles every fourteen months.
- Anthony J. D'Angelo

Suppose that we are wise enough to learn and know - and yet not wise enough to control our learning and knowledge, so that we use it to destroy ourselves? Even if that is so, knowledge remains better than ignorance.
- Isaac Asimov

True, a little learning is a dangerous thing, but it still beats total ignorance.
- Pauline Phillips

The least of the work of learning is done in the classroom.
- Thomas Merton

Good education means learning to read, write and most importantly learn how to learn so that you can be whatever you want to be when you grow up.

— **Patty Murray**

Rich people without wisdom and learning are but sheep with golden fleeces.

— **Solon**

Being really good at 'learning how to learn,' as President Bill Brody of Johns Hopkins put it, will be an enormous asset in an era of rapid change and innovation, when new jobs will be phased in and old ones phased out faster than ever.

— **Thomas Friedman**

You are always learning; there is a lot of grey; don't take things for granted.

— **Lisa Marie Presley**

I think one of the great things about being a musician is that you never stop learning.

— **Yo-Yo Ma**

Life is about learning; when you stop learning, you die.
- **Tom Clancy**

Generally, I like making my own mistakes and learning from them because that's what I think life is about.
- **Taylor Momsen**

If I am through learning, I am through.
- **John Wooden**

I fear the boredom that comes with not learning and not taking chances.
- **Robert Fulghum**

And I believe that the best learning process of any kind of craft is just to look at the work of others.
- **Wole Soyinka**

I grew up going to public school, and they were huge public schools. I went to a school that had 3,200 kids, and I had grade school classes with 40-some kids. Discipline was rigid. Most of the learning was rote. It worked.
- **P. J. O'Rourke**

Everybody who is incapable of learning has taken to teaching.

— **Oscar Wilde**

The only things worth learning are the things you learn after you know it all.

— **Harry S Truman**

I think I started learning lessons about being a good person long before I ever knew what basketball was. And that starts in the home, it starts with the parental influence.

— **Julius Erving**

By playing games you can artificially speed up your learning curve to develop the right kind of thought processes.

— **Nate Silver**

Learning is the new skill. Imagination, creation and asking new questions are at its core.

— **Sugata Mitra**

The soul is everlasting, and its learning experience is lifetime after lifetime.

— **Shirley MacLaine**

In most schools, we measure children on what they know. By and large, they have to memorize the content of whatever test is coming up. Because measuring the results of rote learning is easy, rote prevails. What kids know is just not important in comparison with whether they can think.

- Sugata Mitra

Creative activity could be described as a type of learning process where teacher and pupil are located in the same individual.

- Arthur Koestler

Education should not be about building more schools and maintaining a system that dates back to the Industrial Revolution. We can achieve so much more, at unmatched scale with software and interactive learning.

- Naveen Jain

Always keep learning. It keeps you young.

- Patty Berg

We do not learn; and what we call learning is only a process of recollection.

- Plato

If we want boys to succeed, we need to bring them back to education by making education relevant to them and bring in more service learning and vocational education.

— **Michael Gurian**

I think universities are trying to figure out how we could use what we know about learning to change our education system, but it is sort of funny that they don't necessarily seem to be consulting the people who are sitting right there on campus.

— **Alison Gopnik**

What, of course, we want in a university is for people to learn the skills they're going to need outside the classroom. So, having a system that had more emphasis on inquiry and exploration but also on learning and practising specific skills would fit much better with how we know people learn.

— **Alison Gopnik**

Whether I'm being influenced by new music that I'm listening to, books I've read, my friends, or my faith, I'm learning all the time.

— **Hayley Williams**

One of the things I teach my children is that I have always invested in myself, and I have never stopped learning, never stopped growing.

- Chesley Sullenberger

He who has imagination without learning has wings but no feet.

- Joseph Joubert

Learning is its own exceeding great reward.

- William Hazlitt

Learning is finding out what you already know.

- Richard Bach

I like to think of my behavior in the sixties as a 'learning experience.' Then again, I like to think of anything stupid I've done as a 'learning experience.' It makes me feel less stupid.

- P. J. O'Rourke

Whoso neglects learning in his youth, loses the past and is dead for the future.

- Euripides

Since we can't know what knowledge will be most needed in the future, it is senseless to try to teach it in advance. Instead, we should try to turn out people who love learning so much and learn so well that they will be able to learn whatever needs to be learned.
- **John Holt**

All the time a person is a child he is both a child and learning to be a parent. After he becomes a parent he becomes predominantly a parent reliving childhood.
- **Benjamin Spock**

The main part of intellectual education is not the acquisition of facts, but learning how to make facts live.
- **Oliver Wendell Holmes, Jr.**

Let ignorance talk as it will, learning has its value.
- **Jean de La Fontaine**

I think you're working and learning until you die.
- **J. K. Rowling**

Learning how to learn is life's most important skill.
- **Tony Buzan**

That is what learning is. You suddenly understand something you've understood all your life, but in a new way.
- Doris Lessing

The purpose of learning is growth, and our minds, unlike our bodies, can continue growing as we continue to live.
- Mortimer Adler

The experience gathered from books, though often valuable, is but the nature of learning; whereas the experience gained from actual life is one of the nature of wisdom.
- Samuel Smiles

Learning is always rebellion... Every bit of new truth discovered is revolutionary to what was believed before.
- Margaret Lee Runbeck

There is only one thing more painful than learning from experience and that is not learning from experience.
- Archibald MacLeish

We need to have an educational system that's able to embrace all sorts of minds, and where a student doesn't have to fit into a certain mold of learning.
- **James Hillman**

Strange as it may seem, no amount of learning can cure stupidity, and formal education positively fortifies it.
- **Stephen Vizinczey**

There was a time when young people respected learning and literature and now they don't.
- **Doris Lessing**

Human beings are accustomed to think of intellect as the power of having and controlling ideas and of ability to learn as synonymous with ability to have ideas. But learning by having ideas is really one of the rare and isolated events in nature.
- **Edward Thorndike**

Learning another language is not only learning different words for the same things, but learning another way to think about things.
- **Flora Lewis**

The learning process continues until the day you die.
— **Kirk Douglas**

Recipes tell you nothing. Learning techniques is the key.
— **Tom Colicchio**

You have to learn and keep learning.
— **Gil Scott-Heron**

Teaching is the royal road to learning.
— **Jessamyn West**

Wear your learning like your watch, in a private pocket; and do not pull it out, and strike it, merely to show that you have one.
— **Philip Stanhope, 4th Earl of Chesterfield**

Just as physical exercise is a well-known and well-accepted means to improve health for anyone, regardless of age or background, so can the brain be put 'into shape' for optimal learning.
— **Naveen Jain**

Making distinctions is part of learning. So is making mistakes.
- **Nancy Gibbs**

I hope I'm always learning something.
- **Kate Winslet**

Contrary to current cynicism about past golden ages, the abstraction known as 'the intelligent layperson' does exist - in the form of millions of folks with a passionate commitment to continuous learning.
- **Stephen Jay Gould**

Learning is acquired by reading books, but the much more necessary learning, the knowledge of the world, is only to be acquired by reading men, and studying all the various facets of them.
- **Philip Stanhope, 4th Earl of Chesterfield**

By including children with different learning abilities in mainstream and specialized schools, we can change attitudes and promote respect. By creating suitable jobs for adults with autism, we integrate them into society.
- **Ban Ki-moon**

The top experts in the world are ardent students. The day you stop learning, you're definitely not an expert.
- Brendon Burchard

A little learning is a dangerous thing, but a lot of ignorance is just as bad.
- Bob Edwards

Adults often assume that most learning is the result of teaching and that exploratory, spontaneous learning is unusual. But actually, spontaneous learning is more fundamental.
- Alison Gopnik

The worst mistake you can make with children is to talk to them in a condescending, patronising way and think that you can teach them something. You have to understand that it is you who will be learning from them. You have to get into their world and see things from their perspective.
- Magnus Scheving

I think you never stop learning.
- Norman Foster

Setbacks are just learning experiences.
- **Beth Brooke**

There is no royal road to learning; no short cut to the acquirement of any art.
- **Anthony Trollope**

We learn differently as children than as adults. For grown-ups, learning a new skill is painful, attention-demanding, and slow. Children learn unconsciously and effortlessly.
- **Alison Gopnik**

All are agreed, that the increase of learning and good morals are great blessings to society.
- **Joseph Lancaster**

There's no shortcut to learning a craft; you just have to put the years in.
- **Kylie Minogue**

The introduction of many minds into many fields of learning along a broad spectrum keeps alive questions about the accessibility, if not the unity, of knowledge.
- **Edward Levi**

Learning is the most important thing, no mater how you do it, or where you do it, or who you do it with.
— **Saoirse Ronan**

Attention is the fundamental instrument we use for learning, thinking, communicating, deciding, yet neither parents nor schools spend any time helping young people learn how to manage information streams and control the ways they deploy their attention.
— **Howard Rheingold**

As I enter a new phase of life and my circle broadens, I start learning new things.
— **Kapil Dev**

Learning is what most adults will do for a living in the 21st century.
— **S. J. Perelman**

There is a huge value in learning with instant feedback.
— **Anant Agarwal**

Always keep learning. It keeps you young.
Patty Berg

There is no question that creative intelligence comes not through learning things you find in books or histories that have already been written, but by focusing on and giving value to experience as it happens.

- Antony Gormley

We must expect to fail... but fail in a learning posture, determined no to repeat the mistakes, and to maximize the benefits from what is learned in the process.

- Ted Engstrom

80 percent of learning is visual, so children who can't afford vision correction are at such a disadvantage.

- Ellen Hollman

What I've come to know is that in life, it's not always the questions we ask, but rather our ability to hear the answers that truly enriches our understanding. Never, never stop learning.

- Lester Holt

Learning how to interact with customers is something that anyone starting any business must master. It's an amazing opportunity to be able to learn the ropes at an established company and then employ your expertise at your own company.

- Marc Benioff

Learning can take place in the backyard if there is a human being there who cares about the child. Before learning computers, children should learn to read first. They should sit around the dinner table and hear what their parents have to say and think.

- Dixie Carter

For a small child there is no division between playing and learning; between the things he or she does just for fun and things that are educational. The child learns while living and any part of living that is enjoyable is also play.

- Penelope Leach

Experience is making mistakes and learning from them.

- Bill Ackman

Many think of memory as rote learning, a linear stuffing of the brain with facts, where understanding is irrelevant. When you teach it properly, with imagination and association, understanding becomes a part of it.

- Tony Buzan

I'm still learning, and that's what life is about.

- Cary Elwes

Memory and creativity are essential to education, but if you teach memory incorrectly, it is a total waste of time, and it will inhibit learning.

- Tony Buzan

Some people are so busy learning the tricks of the trade that they never learn the trade.

- Vernon Law

A good part of my leadership skills is crafted from learning from experiences early in my career that were not positive experiences.

- John Lasseter

If you're going to go through hell... I suggest you come back learning something.

- Drew Barrymore

This much I have learned: human beings come with very different sets of wiring, different interests, different temperaments, different learning styles, different gifts, different temptations. These differences are tremendously important in the spiritual formation of human beings.

- John Ortberg

One of the greatest and simplest tools for learning more and growing is doing more.
- **Washington Irving**

I'm constantly learning, and that is the greatest gift of life in my opinion - to always be learning and growing.
- **Kristin Chenoweth**

The extreme sophistication of modern technology - wonderful though its benefits are - is, ironically, an impediment to engaging young people with basics: with learning how things work.
- **Martin Rees**

Directors who turn into big babies and shut out criticism stop learning.
- **Richard King**

I hardly teach. It's more like a gathering of minds looking at one subject and learning from each other. I enjoy the process.
- **Fay Godwin**

The young are adept at learning, but even more adept at avoiding it.

— P. J. O'Rourke

Education is the process in which we discover that learning adds quality to our lives. Learning must be experienced.

— William Glasser

Learning is any change in a system that produces a more or less permanent change in its capacity for adapting to its environment.

— Herbert Simon

Most people stop learning out of fear. They are afraid they cannot learn.

— Henry B. Eyring

I love learning, and I think that curiosity is a wonderful gift.

— Andie MacDowell

I'm still learning, you know. At 80, I feel there is a lot I don't know.

— Lena Horne

What society doesn't realize is that in the past, ordinary people respected learning. They respected books, and they don't now, or not very much. That whole respect for serious literature and learning has disappeared.
- Doris Lessing

Learning from the past helps to ensure that mistakes are not repeated.
- Monica Johnson

The purpose of God's creations and of His giving us life is to allow us to have the learning experience necessary for us to come back to Him, to live with Him in eternal life.
- Henry B. Eyring

By discovering how our minds work, we can improve our learning power and unlock our true potential.
- Robert Winston

I'm happy to be helping people that are passionate about empowering parents for student learning.
- Jeb Bush

I loved education, and, yes, I did want to go on learning.
- Arthur Hailey

It is literally the case that learning languages makes you smarter. The neural networks in the brain strengthen as a result of language learning.
- **Michael Gove**

Learning how to learn is the most precious thing we have in life.
- **John Naisbitt**

A little learning is not a dangerous thing to one who does not mistake it for a great deal.
- **William Allen White**

Of course, learning is strengthened and solidified when it occurs in a safe, secure and normal environment.
- **Jean-Bertrand Aristide**

A huge amount of success in life comes from learning as a child how to make good habits. It's good to help kids understand that when they do certain things habitually, they're reinforcing patterns.
- **Charles Duhigg**

In today's world, learning has become the key to economic prosperity, social cohesion and personal fulfilment. We can no longer afford to educate the few to think, and the many to do.

- David Blunkett

One of the things that is very silly - and I hear from educators all the time - is that schools essentially teach kids to learn. They don't need school for that. Learning is what they do best.

- Ricardo Semler

There is incredible potential for digital technology in and beyond the classroom, but it is vital to rethink how learning is organised if we are to reap the rewards.

- Geoff Mulgan

You should put time into learning your craft. It seems like people want success so quickly, way before they're ready.

- Lucinda Williams

Doing what you do well is death. Your duty is to keep trying to do things that you don't do well, in the hope of learning.

- John Banville

The only thing that mattered was what you were to do in life, and it wasn't about money. It was about teaching, or learning.

- Maya Lin

He that knew all that learning ever writ, Knew only this - that he knew nothing yet.

- Aphra Behn

Children need to be exploring their physical world. They need to be learning the fundamental laws of physics by manipulating objects.

- David Perlmutter

It is undeniable that the best lessons are, and the most learning occurs, when students and the teacher are having fun.

- Robert Jamgotchian

Made in United States
North Haven, CT
07 March 2025